BOUQUET OF HUNGERS

THE UNIVERSITY OF GEORGIA PRESS   ATHENS AND LONDON

BOUQUET OF HUNGERS

BY KYLE G. DARGAN

Image on part openers © iStockphoto.com / Joseph Jean Rolland Dubé

Published by The University of Georgia Press
Athens, Georgia 30602
© 2007 by Kyle G. Dargan
All rights reserved
Designed by Mindy Basinger Hill
Set in 10.5/15 pt Minion Pro
Printed and bound by Thomson-Shore
The paper in this book meets the guidelines for
permanence and durability of the Committee on
Production Guidelines for Book Longevity of the
Council on Library Resources.

Printed in the United States of America

11   10   09   08   07   P   5   4   3   2   1

Library of Congress Cataloging-in-Publication Data

Dargan, Kyle.
  Bouquet of hungers / by Kyle G. Dargan.
      p.   cm.
ISBN-13: 978-0-8203-3031-0 (pbk. : alk. paper)
ISBN-10: 0-8203-3031-0 (pbk. : alk. paper)
1. African Americans—Poetry. I. Title.
PS3604.A74B68 2007
811'.6—dc22   2007015455

British Library Cataloging-in-Publication Data available

I promised to show you a map you say but this is a mural
then yes let it be   these are small distinctions
where do we see it from is the question

ADRIENNE RICH

—

I think I'm getting back to that concept of "dynamic energy."
What you are you don't have to talk about. It shows. With
a feeling of confidence in your movement, truth in it is just
about all you need.

KATHERINE DUNHAM

CONTENTS

Old School Playa to New School Fool: An Author's Note   xi
Acknowledgments   xv

VAMP, BLACK
Ars Poetica   1

(1) PETTY ALCHEMY
Semiotics *or* After the Gangs Came from the West   5
Screen Test, 1965   7
"The heart is the philosopher's stone"   8
Recurring Dream of My Twenties   10
Vagrant Song   11
Eye 1 / eye 2   12
The Exhibit: 1904 World's Fair   13

(2) A FAILURE OF IMAGINATION
Boarding Points   17
Flashback: Invitational   20
Flashback: Background Noise   22
Protest Footage Feat. Suggestions for the President's Daughter   23
Edgar the Security Guard on Poetry   24
George Carlin says   26
Jetsam   28
Untitled   30
Karaoke   31
Newark Boy Assesses Tornado Damage, Weeks Removed   32
Authors Are Not Their Texts   33
Flashback: Wax   34
Assembly Hall   35
Grace on Thee   38
Palinode, Once Removed   39
Letter Home II   40

The Father   41

Still Life w/ President, Wreath, and Unknown Soldier   42

Orange   43

Quagmire   45

(3) THE GUEST PREACHER

Dukkha   49

Every End   50

The Calling   51

Sex Ed   52

Censorship Psalm   53

Emaciation   54

Sermon   55

(4) GROUND UP

Elegy for "The Fair One"   59

Tour   60

Caliban   61

Eye Wading   63

Letter Home I   64

Train Dialogue   65

Shade Tree   66

Sightseeing I: Prefab   67

Shedding a Pimp   68

Boy Dies Falling   69

Sightseeing II   70

NOTICE: To the Addict Who Robbed Us on a Landscaping Job   71

(5) THE POST-SOUL PAPERS

Folk [affirmativeambivalence]   75

1980   76

Tesserae   77

Phat: A Metadiscourse on the Value of Canonizing the Round
   (Spheropygian), Broad (Platypygous), and Bulging (Pleopygian)
   Buttocks (with a Resistance to Such Speech)   79
McCollards   81
Martin Luther King, Jr., and His Family: Paper Dolls   83

VAMP, BLUE
Piccolo BLACK ART   87

Notes   91

OLD SCHOOL PLAYA TO NEW SCHOOL FOOL

AN AUTHOR'S NOTE

I met a gypsy and she hipped me to some life game
To stimulate then activate the left and right brain
Said "baby boy, you only funky as your last cut
You focus on the past, your ass'll be a has-what"

ANDRÉ BENJAMIN

Two years ago, while driving home for the summer from Indiana, my roommate and I were traveling up the ruthless monotony that is the Pennsylvania Turnpike, and as we emerged from the last land tunnel before the I-81 junction, my phone began to vibrate in my pocket. To our surprise, it was a very late, though welcome, call about a scholarship to attend the Fine Arts Work Center. So, two months later, I was on a high-speed ferry crossing Massachusetts Bay, eagerly awaiting the opportunity to set foot on what I believed was the farthest one can walk on contiguous U.S. soil into the Atlantic ocean.

Until then, most of what I'd experienced of isolation had been social, ideological, or cultural in nature—I've never been in a place where I was hurting for *land*. But after checking into the work center and, within two days, successfully walking the tip of the peninsula from coast to coast, I felt I had exhausted Provincetown. In actuality, there was probably much to explore within the town center, but inside the town I was very much the outsider being neither well-to-do nor white . . . nor gay (though, having recently left Indiana, it was reassuring to be in a place seemingly absent of the impetus for people to conceal from public that aspect of their beings).

Feeling othered and twice cramped in this beautiful little town, I desired to find a space where I could dig myself out from under the weight of difference and stake off some mental terrain I could inhabit. So while out on a night walk, I happened upon a used bookstore towards the end of Commercial Street. It had a keen balance of order and entropy: genres sectioned off nicely, while the individual shelves contained some degree of alphabetical chaos. Somewhere among the upper tiers of the poetry section, surely not the H's, I found a copy of Suheir Hammad's *Born Palestinian, Born Black*—a book, a poet, I had heard of often but rarely encountered in physical form. (Since then, I've been lucky enough to cross paths with her on a number of occasions, at least twice while waiting for the PATH train back to Jersey from WTC—staring at her for a few minutes before deciding to whisper, "Suheir?") I thumbed the unevenly cut pages until I reached the Author's Note. I was, I'm ashamed to say, shocked and intrigued by the idea because I had been so firmly reared in the "art need not explain itself (save for the purpose of facilitating critique)" school. Immediately, that concept seemed like bunk—of course a writer could provide context for a work without it reading like play-by-play.

Hammad, who as a young girl moved with her family from Beirut to the United States, begins her note by saying, "Home is with me. I carry everyone and everything I am with me wherever I go. Use my history as the road in front of me, the land beneath me." While I carried many things into the writing of this book, I give you this warning about the text in your hands: "place" and "history" are the main adversaries of this being a book—a book in the sense of contiguous experience. Do not let the places fool you, as the names of places and the notions they carry mean nothing until you've been to those places, breathed or suffocated there. This book is as vacillating as I was during the time I was writing these poems, a time during which I was living in various parts of the country and finding my maps of the country's physical, social, and intellectual topography needed to be constantly redrawn.

As far as history is concerned, during the process of writing this book I began asking myself what it means to work in the black tradition and what it means to be a black writer. I have always identified the black tradition with a feeling that black people in America carry the burden of bearing witness—not just to truth and to the abuses or violations of universal rights over the eras but also to the burden of having to "bear witness to," to forecast, possible futures where America the concept begins to achieve its full potential. For a people to fight and deliver themselves from enslavement to citizenship, they would have had to possess a collective imagination mighty enough to resist the debilitating realities that filled their eyes and ears. This imagination, I embrace.

The second question is more slippery, but I think I've decided that, for myself, to be a black writer means nothing more than that I am black and I write. Yes, there is a tradition, a history, implied—one that I am beholden to. But we must be wary of labels that—aesthetically, thematically, or otherwise—dictate more than they inspire, that serve as content controls rather than content facilitators, that help sell books more than they help create them. The age of "Black is" has passed. This book is written in the age of "black does," and though history still acts as a road beneath and before me, it also begs that the road be improvised, remade, and renewed—that it be allowed to act more as the thoroughfare from which an infinite number of avenues can branch.

To that effect, this work is arranged more like some of my favorite albums than a book. While many have suggested to me that *The Listening* was a "musical" text, I feel there is much more of what I have learned from listening in this book. *Songs in the Key of Life, De La Soul Is Dead, Aquemini, Voodoo, Mama's Gun, Electric Circus, The Headphone Masterpiece, Blend Crafters, The Love Below, The New Danger, Tennessee Slim Is the Bomb, The Shining, St. Elsewhere, Game Theory*—these albums were all on repeat while this bouquet came together because they each exhibit an aesthetic diversity that speaks to creative curiosity and, as a result, expand the boundaries and weaken the perceived limitations of their respective genres. Though they may not have had an intended audience at the time of their release, they each created one and an ensuing appetite for more.

The Author
January 19, 2007
Washington, D.C.

ACKNOWLEDGMENTS

Versions of these poems first appeared in the following publications:

"Quagmire" in *Bat City Review*; "Ars Poetica," "Newark Boy Assesses Tornado Damage, Weeks Removed," and "Phat" in *Callaloo*; "Shade Tree" in *Shenandoah*; and "Jetsam" in *Warpland*.

"1980," "Emaciation," "Quagmire," "Piccolo BLACK ART," "Screen Test, 1965," and "Tour" are featured on *From the Fishouse: An Audio Archive of Emerging Poets* (http://www.fishousepoems.org).

"Boarding Points," "Grace on Thee," "Still Life w/ President, Wreath, and Unknown Soldier," and "Tesserae" are featured on *Beltway Poetry Quarterly* (http://washingtonart.com/beltway/contents.html).

"Folk," "Letter Home II," "NOTICE," and "Semiotics" are featured on *MiPOesias Magazine* (http://www.mipoesias.com).

"Censorship Psalm," "Karaoke," "Recurring Dream of My Twenties," "Sermon," and "Shade Tree" were featured on the *National Literary Review* (http://www.nationalliteraryreview.org/poetry.htm).

Many thanks to all who either provided or pointed me towards the blooms assembled here as well as those who helped sustain me as I journeyed from one place to the next. I am grateful for the financial and/or professional support of the following organizations and institutions: the Bread Loaf Writers' Conference, the Bucknell Young Writers Seminar, the Cave Canem Foundation, the Fine Arts Work Center, and Indiana University. Special thanks to Jericho Brown, Rita Dove, John McCluskey, Alyce Miller, Charles Rowell, Sara Jane Stoner, and Kevin Young for helping to shape the manuscript over three years.

ARS POETICA

Stone John wasn't prone to ruckus,
just running—letters branded on his cheeks
from his first flight. Soft jewels,
toes, and an ear lopped clean off and mounted
on the stable posts after a second, a third.
Fourth try, he gimped his way past the limits,
stood there, inhaled faux free air to know
it could be done, and floated on back. So was John—
kindling angst within his family, keeping the slavers
honest as scripture. Fifth time, pateroller
caught John amongst the pines and there
he refused to give the hunter any more flesh
or weather his family's salty tongues.
He straightened up and turned to rock—
jagged skin tearing chunks from the whip,
form too heavy for men or mules to haul. In
the woods, winds made John hum sweetly
and people brought ears. Stone John stands
in a museum up south now. He is loved
—his glass quarters kept so clean.

(1) PETTY ALCHEMY

SEMIOTICS *OR* AFTER GANGS CAME FROM THE WEST

The graphite of winter hedges
stuffed with sparrows and rustling

trash gives way to the three o'clock
flood of little suns escaping the globes

and algebra books that orbit them
all day. They clot on corners, claiming rival

hues of hemoglobin. They bounce-walk
and break into an origami of bone—

fold their hands into birds, fingers flapping
and preening. A red feather tags

danger, as does blue—what irrigates
their bodies so dooms them. It seems

affectionate enough at first—chatty
hands and hugs that end in thumps

on backs—but a darker exchange ensues
when one sun is red, the other blue,

when bird hands dive below waists
to emerge with fire in their beaks.

Someteen, these young suns set with their light
splattered about the bushes—

a cold ignition of color. We blot it
with stuffed bears and wind-scarred roses

until leaves migrate back to branches—
spring's green shroud saying *forgive me,*

you shouldn't have to see this.

SCREEN TEST, 1965

AFTER ANDY WARHOL

Four severe minutes. Every absent
color in the world coalesces
in the left hand of these frames—
a black half-veil. It is unclear
where the poet's face survives
the shadow. The face
pivots left (its left)
and light holds a line
at the nose while darkness, wounded, eats
the cheek and much of the eye
socket—the gorged
right eye set free to lumber
its way off the face
into some ommetaphobe's
blinded sleep. Ask now
if the art has consciousness.
I would shout yes if it wasn't
Ashbery—the '65
model of that face he makes
where everything 'cept those eyes
numbs into a mum abstraction.

"THE HEART IS THE PHILOSOPHER'S STONE"

which we then took
to mean the thinking

man moves unanchored—lithe,
having excised the dead-

weight stowed in the thorax.
The body believed

in the heart enough to cup
it with hollow slabs of blood

and air. The futility of feeling
fools to the thinking man—the blind

one who cast decisions by listening
to his stone or others with gravel,

too many small hearts chattering
and confusing the body.

The primacy—pulse and heat—all stones long
for. A heart is too stubborn

to be a stone—without desire, just
a throbbing that knows to throb in time

with bioelectric ticks: each a mere encore
of the sourceless first. Heart—its failure

so precious, the things we set
between lungs' approximate

embrace, even thoughts of them,
tend to yield some sallow gold.

RECURRING DREAM OF MY TWENTIES

The grounds at war again. I still breathe
by the grace of a wild green
horse—a landslide of hoof and muscle
—whose sheen seduces rain
from explosion-pocked skies. The haze of falling
water presses against war's fog
until the mist around me is all
the snipers can slay.
                              Our daily route,
we bring new word to the front
line and return with heaps of shattered man
tied down to the mustang's hips.

The more fighting, the more adrenaline
thaws from fear into joy   and our green
and brown blur—a man's gut against
a horse's bowed spine—is the music of being
more than surviving, of moving
too fast to smell the death we tow or read
the meticulously rolled notes from generals
detailing how more are to be felled.

VAGRANT SONG

RIPTON, VERMONT

I watch a man walk home with a bowl-cut boy
on his shoulders—his frame epic despite
the small feat. Their Airedale terrier,
tethered to a line crossing the yard,
begins her welcome—a boisterous prance
among mountains blue with evening
and gorged with echoes of her woof.

Then it is quiet, the absent tone
bearded men keep their beards for
and level land within axe-reach.
A homestead to come—all necessary
trunks torn from the forest cresting
these flat indexes of green.

Modernity, as if tethered to the black
wires threaded high through the woods,
rumbles up the dirt—
all rubber and combustion.
                                        I want to see
this place bitter, bury notions
that this lack of air is what we seek.
Thinly, I chant "O, skyline" like a mirror
spell to protect against my softening,
only to realize this fight I've picked again,
where brick against bark is never
a worthy debate. The far ridge's last line
leaps into the foreground's sponged foliage—
I it let go. Feeling the tether on my leg, I turn
to seek the stone I'm indebted to—
asphalt, the goddamned
road that always manages to find me.

EYE 1 / EYE 2

I am a soft
spoken blade
thousand serrations
for every decibel of
its hum
I am going to cut you
bleeding will be
your choice   I thank you
in advance   red
tongues spilling over
your body
I've no interest to see
your flesh: think pink
think my flesh: see pink cells
think Pavlovian windows
to the show   fluids
never miss a curtain
calling   none of this is act
is you   the world
is an eye before
a stage

braille transcription of
light's serpenting through irises'
sunken novas   a sublime hurt
thought   the sketched brain   machinal
this nondance   watch
(which is the hardest step)
contrapuntal   your reasons
for seeing my need to replace your crystal balls
wrists and digits   riddling their convex conjure
chin and breast in refute   too full
as though the world crawls from it   a world
where exists such an *I* that to be seen is to brand
unrecognizable   the body once one then two
the body filming itself
action   inside a harnessed reaction
color the reels   mere shadow lies
of stars red-shifting only after
the body's fleeting memory
will matter least once man is restored
achieving vision
inchoate   beginning

THE EXHIBIT: 1904 WORLD'S FAIR

ST. LOUIS, MISSOURI

It is a dismal sight to see those
savages kill (we murder from necessity,
they to appease some primitive will).
N. J. LOFTIS

This invisible cage pulses, a piece-
wise lung—these flesh bars, my space
staked by how close they dare circle.

Again a photographer flashes me
running stones across the ends
of brittling branches. I imagine
the caption: *savage prepares*
for hunt. What prey
wouldn't see me coming in this
forged nature, my skin no more hidden
than the torch that moves against twilight?

I have a small pyre and a hut
whose hay crest would stop
no inspired rain. There is one
Geronimo—a fellow display—
who was not named by white men.
All day the Apache signs folios and passes
outside his arrowheaded shack.
His signature, I hear, earns him
upwards of twenty cents.
The modest and poor flutter around me,
disappointed I don't favor
caricatures and skull diagrams
from their monthlies and heralds.

Men here are called "Adam"—chosen
shepherds of their god, yet
the right to give me name
they claim from sciences. A matter
of numbers, their heads deemed able to capture
more. Their maps mark soul as resting
from the neck up, but I know
the deafening sight of it around me
and how to breathe, welcome it
throughout this body.

(**2**) A FAILURE
OF IMAGINATION

BOARDING POINTS
BUS STATION, NE D.C.

[N]

A baby is one less
bag you may carry.

[E]

The hustler's faded velour,
a tepid, alien hide—let him
take you home.

[S]

The New York direct, ever punctual
as it is never arriving
from anywhere. It grows
out of the tarmac, wet to steaming.

[W]

"Hey poet, you got any papers?"
Shouldn't papers be laced with poems?

[S]

Some idle stiller than the coaches.

[E]

"I can't. At the department store
today, I bought a face. I owe them
this spare change."

[W]

When the busses stop,
these men will clean up
into princes, igniting night like
Montecristos kissed by razors.

[N]

The brother with the shakes
is suspicious of the bench.
He may be on to something.

[S]

The longest line: WILLIAMSBURG,
HAMPTON, NORFOLK, VIRGINIA BEACH.
Somewhere, coasts remember
the first vessel.

[E]

Industry: now
the beggar has a soda
and a straw.

[*W*]

The new shift at the ticket booth
wears a cotton phallus from her neck.
Over the p.a., she tames crowds.

[*S*]

Thunk—an infant Newton
jostles receivers from pay
phones' palms onto his skull.
Even against babies
there are laws.

FLASHBACK: INVITATIONAL
BLAIR ACADEMY, BLAIRSTOWN, NEW JERSEY

They never come to us,
the pine-garnished prep schools. Color
only on their pristine hardwood courts.
Our headmaster releases us early—eager
that we travel thirty or forty miles
and meet our competition.
St. Benedict's cross-country,
a Jamaican bobsled team of running—
our best legs, a yardboy named Flonsdale;
Hicks, the rolling keystone;
I, the silent, brooding captain;
Coach, the brown Sun Tzu—mental
in his approach to duels of legs.

His plan is simple: get out
fast, break all takers in the first mile—
Hicks will pull the middle,
Flons and I stretch the pack, and the freshmen
add some flavor to the stragglers.
We warm up, think *quick feet*, and touch
our pastry-thin shoes to the chalk line.
Nerves leak Freon, coach keeps us focused.
Watch for the smoke and go.
The gun releases its plume, and we are in motion
before the sound lances our ears.

The blob of runners molds into a gaggle.
Bound to Flons, I settle towards the apex.
Keeping pace around the golf course
and up into the woods, we separate
like tomato seeds from the slime cavity—
capping off the rope of runners as the path narrows.
It came from the trees, an arrow,
"Catch those niggers!" The pacer in my chest
forgets its one-two. A moment
later the beat resumes, but now
it is too late for reflex—
Flonsdale has already decided to run harder.

FLASHBACK: BACKGROUND NOISE
UNIVERSITY OF VIRGINIA

Over the summer, our lone white suitemate
guided tours through the FBI headquarters.
The bureau would call us before break,
standard background checks. They posed

"Now does Mr. Fox have any Arab
friends?" I said "No." I wanted to say "No . . .

well, Rasul and Ahmed come over
on Thursdays—toking apricot tobacco
smoke from the hookah,
always talking about infidels and shit."

But I couldn't stomach the joke. Brian actually
needed his job. So "no," though a door over Shagon
was backsliding with Bihar—a Persian girl
who would've fit their eager descriptions.

PROTEST FOOTAGE FEAT. SUGGESTIONS
FOR THE PRESIDENT'S DAUGHTER

MOBBED, MANHATTAN

Someone is holding a sign: DRAFT JENNA.
Dwarfed by downtown's architecture,
to decode this block font is my plummet—innards
erecting themselves in my torso, the planet faltering
briefly. I fear the poet's means of eating
—the violence of each render
(the first week of war, debris
on Baghdad palms, I saw snow). Must the poem
that beds with the ugly now awake to mobs
sinking in their anticauses, begging
it grant them buoyancy, begging it regress
to the bias all speech dissolves in? Let this be
a letter to my Jenna—

Dear Jenna,
what if they force fatigues on you? Democracy
aside, I believe it is a frightened man
who champions more women in war.
Then again, I am still the scared one
here—people are already pulling your card.

EDGAR THE SECURITY GUARD ON POETRY
COLLEGE STATION, TEXAS

Smoked every brand out there.
These, a dollar fifty, taste no different
than the Benson & Hedges I gave years to.
I am no hero, unlike
the friends I buried over there

—

After my field commission,
I never lost another man. My grip
shook from deployment to the hop
home. Couldn't give up
cigarettes after that. I'm sixty-seven
and only read on the job. I need
words that keep me sharp.
This Welsh guy, he writes about combat
in language that makes war
sound like sheet music. There was
no melody—I had to silence small shadows
smuggling munitions for the gooks.
I did my duty, provided
for a wife and seven kids

—

So, they wouldn't give me rank
until I went back to school. I had to read
poetry. All the "thees" and "thous" and "flowers"—
I'd fall asleep. I've never understood
war, the need is just over my head.
I like mysteries—Mosley's good,
but I'll try this Song of Napalm. *I knew fire,*
but it never sounded like music

GEORGE CARLIN SAYS

EN ROUTE, TEXAS

either you pray to god
or Joe Pesci. Point: with either,
half the time you will be heard while
half your pleas will burn in flight.

I've decided to clutch
Man of the People to my stomach
and have faith Chinua Achebe
will get me back to the ground.

My last lift off, I was "little guy," now it's "*Sir*,
would you like a pillow." My eyes refuse
the soft, meshy sedative—
watching as the plane peels away.

Dallas shrivels to an organic motherboard—
vehicles moving like bytes,
our information moving like air. Higher,
I reread the shape of scattered clouds

from above—porous rows unravel
below wings. The plane content in its altitude,
my hands loosen to crack the bound spine
and I recall Achebe speaking. The story of Tortoise—

the sly shellback who (1) got the birds to loan him feathers
(2) took on the name "You all" and (3) was the only one
allowed to eat when they reached the sky feast
(*You all may eat*). The birds repossessed his plumage,

leaving him up here as a reminder,
do not deceive the sky or its disciples. Tortoise
learning too when entering the earth's attic,
we can only grab hold of a ripe boll and hope

the ground will be kind next time you meet.

JETSAM

Folks done upset the old man river,
made him carry slave ships and fed him dead niggas.
MOS DEF

I learned to sink in Rahway pool,
facing up and forcing air out
until the coarse floor set
against my back like a lost anemone
or some synthetic coral.

        Currents, hear me.
By the time you settled,
the yearning was flushed
from your lungs—your wind already
joining with the underwater breezes
choreographing global climate.
We know this, yet speak our prayers
towards the other blue plane.
While your spirit lies in sediment,
is it arrogant of us
to think of paradise as up? The sky
is an echo of cotton,
yet most long for its promise.

Whole, we are a mountain hauled
across seas—your shards sacrificed
to ensure a cargo. America was a quarry
drawn to grind us apart. Heart is the rain
that pounds, calls us to rivers—fresh
water dendrites over the land. They flood
and ache, begging homecoming.

Within, we remember
how you all met the salt water. Salt
and hull splinters on our tongues, we are quiet
among a trader-race who thinks
we don't swim as well as we fly.

UNTITLED

Would it matter if I told you "it was
a damned and vehement billowing"—

far worse than when sentry angels fumbled
the first flaming sword into new oceans

en route to god's garden. Maybe
the garden is more important here:

dark creation, what I saw in the steam's exponential
desire. Each new miniplume threatening to form

a head, then a cylindrical torso, then stunted
footstool limbs until the old serpent was reborn—
primed to breathe the flames extinguished
by refineries' borrowed river water. *Wait,*
why would the end of humanity start here—
the hamstrung joint of Indiana and Illinois?

Smell the grit in the air. Why not?

KARAOKE

Here's to back-riffs, the Japanese, naval
baseball caps, pack-a-day rasp, thanking god
for being a boy, a country, tonight (no liquor
sold on Sundays), cracking the fire
exit, the Beethoven cellular opus
stubborn as a canker sore, Tom (going once,
going twice . . .), contagious slow dancing
in the kitchen entrance, yellow tint spilling through
the white lyrics, '80s catalogs, hands colliding
a beat too late, contemplating Lou Rawls,
forcarm hair, STIHL patches, Stars
and Bars pulsing on pickup windows
in the dirt lot, Indiana, Johnny
      Cash and *believing*
that the lord was on their side, sunset
drawl, three-drink makeovers, (instrumental
break), men in each other's blank
embrace, cigarette burns
and no pain, Bette Midler
and chorus mentality, stripes
really making you feel thinner,
playing the air guitar like a penis
and redmen singing western, the last pair
of Levi's stitched in the States,
America the plaid, saliva forgotten, and *the soldiers
coming home*. Maybe next Wednesday I sing.

NEWARK BOY ASSESSES TORNADO DAMAGE, WEEKS REMOVED

MARTINSVILLE, INDIANA

These trees bent like gleaners over the road—
foam insulation blooming
on cracked, skinned branches—this is
what happens when wind riots.
The whites do not fly
to farther suburbs. They keep
their half-homes—men zip up flannel lumberjacks,
climb ladders, breathe sawdust.
Women make beds, tuck in alyssum,
unskew arborvitaes. Soon,
the town's face is reconstructed,
if not restored. The mêlée
remembered only in dirt—
where city and country disagree.

AUTHORS ARE NOT THEIR TEXTS

CHICAGO, ILLINOIS

Dear James [Baldwin],

Saw you at Borders today. They managed
to fit all of you in AFRICAN-AMERICAN
LITERATURE. One shining corner—barely any room
left after all the girlfriend fiction had been stocked.

I didn't move the copy of *Giovanni's Room*
but ferried everything else over to LITERATURE/
FICTION. The women with their creeping ladders
stopped me, said there wasn't space
in literature. I pressed you into the bookshelf
until pages buckled—what is considered damage.
They charged me to buy them all, so I charged.

Toni Cade Bambara watched from the shelf
below as books flanking your hole caved in.

FLASHBACK: WAX

FRANKLIN ELEMENTARY SCHOOL (NOW WHITNEY HOUSTON
ACADEMY), EAST ORANGE, NEW JERSEY

Who wasn't relieved
when the art teacher
phased out the finger-
thick generic crayons,
putting "flesh" colored
Crayolas in our hands?
I always colored
with brown, remorseful
for the few kids who'd point
sister, mommy, dad at dark
construction paper figures
filled in with the old
brilliant blankness. How
did their parents survive it—
who could ever live up
to being cast that white?

ASSEMBLY HALL

> *sun man get up rise heart of universes to be*
> *future of the world*
> AMIRI BARAKA

I

You best me here, Indiana—
                    America minus
its patch of stars
—asphyxiating unity,
harsh binary of crimson and cream.
My last resort, I sit—
a kamikaze stillness as seats snap
back and bodies rise to our Star Spangled Banner.
One of 17,257, mite
on the scalp of a doomed beast—
torso of an elephant, legs of an ass.
How can I hurt you?

II

Look around.
Sun-man coaches this team.
Sun-man tosses
cheerleaders like sandbags.
Sun-men hustle tickets outside.
A sun-woman picks tickets at the gate.
You sun-men lining the courtside,
who could they pull from this crowd
to fill your eleven jerseys?

III

The retarded man in the next seat,
the one who only stands if he sees his brother
doing the same, knows to clap and shout
Go I-U . . . Fight, Fight, Fight into his palms
when bands start up during time-outs.
He reminds me of those boys, fraternity
brothers in an SUV, shouting *Jihad, Jihad, Jihad*—
emptying their imaginary m-16's into me
as I walked down Kirkwood towards simpler slaughter.

IV

In the age of flag, I stand—
bent to my own futility.

In the age of flag,
god blesses the country
and counts his losses.

In the age of flag,
we don't exist.

V

To keep Hoosier basketball
games enjoyable (possible for all),
we ask that you respect the norms around you.
If a patron displays conduct that disorients
coaches, officials, or other patrons, Indiana
University reserves the right
to absorb said individual into Assembly Hall.
No refunds will be given in such cases.

GRACE ON THEE

Soon the pretty machines will want you
to touch them, to point (appoint)
another man leader. Speak a fingerprint
language to the touch screen's plastic
membrane: "he's . . . the one." Like solar sails,
pretty machines need nothing tactile
to run—not a finger or brain or fear-
of-god. The pretty machines can cast their own
decisions but want you to press and leave
grease smudges on their bloodless skin—to make
you think there's a rib in there somewhere.
You want to believe some Gepetto somewhere
knew he had ribs, knew he was unlike
the pretty machines he was crafting. Pretty
machines know there's no return to their predecessors—
those analog, beige box-bots with ballot tabs sloped
against us, suspicious as brows, and levers
that wheezed a record of every hope.

PALINODE, ONCE REMOVED

BLOOMINGTON, INDIANA

> *The Negro is America's metaphor*
> RICHARD WRIGHT

The girl from Martinsville sets her eyes on me
like they are elbows—intently boring
at my cheeks. This sentiment bleeds
throughout my class. Slouched, heads
tilted, they wait for the day I come in,
pull out a handkerchief, a vial of alcohol,
and wipe this vexing complexion from my skin.

Before I left home, Uncle called—said,
"You're going to teach *them* people, huh?
Well, teach 'em."

The day we pursue metaphor, I will
teach them about the brain—how there is a center
to catch discrepancy between the expected
and the perceived. Stimulate the mechanism,
you are working in metaphor.

                                    Though surprising
I am not a metaphor. This is: I am a period,
small and dark. If you read me correctly,
you are to stop. Pause. Breathe.

LETTER HOME II

VIA BLOOMINGTON, INDIANA

The trees, on the flank the wind beats,
are scabbed with snow.

Tell Grandmother not to worry—
I've met a nice girl in the library. She isn't us,
but I'll ask her out. Expect grandchildren

soon. People shrink in the cold. Momma,
I imagine you may be as tall as me again.

THE FATHER

AFTER BROOKS

To be in love
is to touch things with a lighter hand.

Know this of me—I loved
her, all. Loved
the anomaly of you
who did not have form—bright
gnarl of tissue on the inner
hull. Yes, you could have traveled
with us (you do carry
with us). This ball
we bounced and stilled,
the floating throb of unresolved
energy, because . . . because . . .

I muse
as though you can hear—
denied spirit, off
to another body-gate.

You are the beautiful half
of a golden hurt,

so let her hate me today for never
having to know the remnant
blood in carnal seams. Your
silence never lets me forget her.
I believe mine was love
for her, with and without.

STILL LIFE W/ PRESIDENT,
WREATH, AND UNKNOWN SOLDIER

NOVEMBER 11, 2004

He would second that it is god's work
to define infinities within the boundary of stone.

Bygone and unaccounted for, this
single warrior grows colossal before him—

distended from being fed the legs, torsos,
names of those we are too human, too desirous
of divinity, to admit we will never know
how they moved from our bit of known world.

We place them all here and drum the good things,
drum their service—how they left clearer

the turbid human condition, smoothed
over unmarked graves of chaparral, ocean, or ridge.
Wreath in hand, he bends penitently over the marble
tomb—gingerly as though it once housed a mine.

ORANGE

FEBRUARY 14, 2003

Colin Powell slipped into our high school unannounced—
eight in the morning, 520 boys and
a handful of monks with habits draping their thin backs.
We always had to be on time. Father Ed said,
"If I can make it, so can you"—when *make* meant crossing
his ten steps between school and monastery.
All this amidst talk of first black president.
No camera crews or *Star-Ledger* reporters, who would expect
EX-GENERAL VISITS BENEDICTINES IN CENTRAL WARD.
Some teachers knew. Sparse flashes bloomed, wilted,
capturing his breadth while he marched in Shanely gym—
haulting to pivot on the garnet-gray "B."
He looked crisper in his blue suit, not puffy
or drab as in full camouflage 1600 Penn. press
conferences. He talked halfway into second period—
what I remember is his story of falling
into what looked like ground and piercing his foot
on edged bamboo blessed with dung; his foot
converted, turned purple and ripe as the jungle,
before they sent him home.

Today, I imagine the foot pulses when he sits
before the UN. I half trust him, not the man
he speaks for, the man who pulls him from the cabinet
like a setting for valued guests. Who can trust
antiwar protests will pierce minds, or that Shock
and Awe (sixty elephants worth
of cruise missiles, forty-eight hours, crippling
Iraqi morale) will excavate
our threat? Who bets on al-Qaeda grading U.S. soil
again? What's worth a bomb or nerve

43

toxin here in Indiana? For the first time in thirty years
the EBS's whine would not be warm-up—fifty miles
south of Indy I'll be without reception, without cable.
I trust family on the Atlantic can't afford $6,000
gas suits or $9,000 tents to halt radiation
for nine days. I trust The Administration
will have missile defense systems up and humming
in time. I trust blue yellow green will be retired,
living only orange or red. Black, white lose
implication when in a second this could be dust.
No united atoms or flecks of Middle East. World dust—
like that. If I snap my fingers, such light
takes even less time to level than it takes sound
to leave my skin. I believe Malcolm
when he warned chickens come
home to roost. The old world ruffles
its wings. It snows, and the snow,
it falls like feathers.

QUAGMIRE

PROVINCETOWN, MASSACHUSETTS

Forget the lily pads angled
up out the water, green lids
insects gnaw like winged goats.

Forget the hawk, who probably thinks
the feeling mutual.
Forget the pine needle garnishes,
gnats bounding the pond's skin,
mosquitoes engrossed in bloody games of tag.

Matter of fact, forget green—
the way it proliferates, the way
it sways, reaches, turns brown.

Forget the sky's false blue,
light's refraction due
to the angle it strikes atmosphere.

Forget water, forget order—
how biology all makes sense
if you live long enough:

the frog gulps the fly, the bird
sucks back the frog, sediment
and maggots claim the dead bird, the seed
feeds off the dirt, the tree nests
the bird that eyes the frog.

The cycle—the zero sum—the reason we build coffins.

(3) THE GUEST
PREACHER

DUKKHA

The Buddha said, "I teach one thing
and one thing only: suffering and the end of suffering"

Tongs ascend from turbulent grease
with two crisped whiting—silver undersides
pressed together and clothed with white bread.
This is the offering
we bring Aunt Laura. *The noble*
truth of the origin of suffering is this:

We've had our weekly argument over what
she shouldn't ingest, whether it matters
at this point. *It is the thirst which produces*
re-existence, re-becoming. Boldly,
my grandmother carries the bag
between the rehab orderlies—resolved
her sister's health or happiness is beyond
workings of their hands. *Thirst*

for sense-pleasures. Every week,
where she is less, there is more food
untouched. *Thirst for non-existence.*
The sandwich is too large
a structure. We break it knowing
to do so is duty, and the sweet
sodium will lead her towards either end.

EVERY END

An ant exits the sky onto my shoulder.
No iron wings or stretched pinions
for an eye's length above, the sky is a bare
tablecloth awaiting trimmings.

For some there is no egg—
no womb nor pouch
nor amnion of rebirth.
They simply drop from the horizon
like crates of rations
shoved off the curbs of heaven.

The black asterisk is crawling
across the limbo of my white shirt.
*Who were you, your previous
name—can you remember? I'll call you
Samuel*, brushing the ant from my sleeve,
christened with the back of my hand, hoping
it floats down to the weed-flanked drag.

THE CALLING

I open the door for Mormons trekking
through our weary neighborhood,
not seeking new religion or painfully
interested in what they'll say. I hear them.
They are young blond men—short-sleeve
dress shirts, black ties, and backpacks stuffed
with salvation—stationed in this city
where young guns ache for reasons to release.
Vividly other, they believe in something
enough to risk a walk down Freeway Drive
crisp as targets. *What do you believe in?*
They call me, spiritual mercenary, to answer.
People are able to pour faith in many vessels.
When the right thing ask we leave our doors
open, I believe we will be ready.

SEX ED

While monks convene—five minutes
every Wednesday morning
after convocation—we young boys sit
in rooms with crotchety radiators,
waiting to be taught The Word.

There's gossip about who's being recruited,
debate of top ten emcees of all time,
traded theories on why
the Knicks will never win another one—
shouldn't have signed Houston
for the big money.
A twenty-two-inch TV/VCR hybrid
mounted above the blackboard
temps as an authority figure.

Fatir, whose attendance column
reads like a totem of L's, darts through
the pistachio-green room with a black rectangle
that he slides into the set's mouth.
His hands slap POWER, PLAY, and he's gone
snickering down the hall.

Out of fuzz and sound like hard rain comes
brown bodies. It looks like birth—
screams and sweat on skin.
But something is going in, two briars of hair
mash each other as the camera pans out.
Father Matthew steps into class, his hair made
whiter by the sound. We boys want to fly,
sing out *Fatir did it*, but none move—
each arrested in learning how

CENSORSHIP PSALM

A shame we all enter the world dressed
provocatively. Barely hair-clad,
like bodies that lead eyes
to bear false witness—
our L's so misplaced, arteries mis-
wire and pump to the groin
blood meant for the heart.

—

Who are we to judge whole-
some arousal, the likes of which signs sex
with childbirths embedded in the commercial
breaks (and now we return to—a baby,
a family already in progress)?

—

Years after we never kissed, I discovered
both my fourth-grade girlfriend and I wondered
if you raised a man and a woman
in a white box closed to the world,
would they know to *know* each other. Of course,
they wouldn't—we are not to be piqued
until He says "go forth." Thus, bless
the censors, their black bars and silence
purging our static, the cataract-
cloudy world, until it's clear enough
to discern that leveling whisper: "*Yes, you
and you, I say it is now safe to rise.*"

EMACIATION

I keep thinking you can't eat god. You can't eat god—his second four will consume him because you can't eat god. The billboard along the interstate asks LOOKING FOR A SIGN FROM GOD? Half a mile later: HERE IT IS—both backgrounds clean as china. Another sign: GOT FAITH?— water from a faucet ferments to burgundy gold upon crossing the lips of a goblet. At the core of Indiana, people hunger beyond vocabulary. *I'm hungry* pronounced "God hates." In the middle of the workweek, the hungry men clamor through campus growling "God hates fags." Smites them. Sows fire beneath Mohammed. Awaits murderers of innocence—contradictions wild as ulcers blooming in their bellies. And I kept mumbling "people can't eat god." You can't eat god. He will get his seconds because he feeds these people god—a bread not meant for the belly skews the body's fullness, the body that walks everyday and does the work of god. And these hungry people belt "God hates, God Hates"—the bloody fetus on their placards like a body, like bad bread, and bleeding faucets flow on billboards. If these bodies hate, it is because they've known hunger for half a century and every fourth year the ballot brought them little bread. They cap their ears, tilt chins up—tongues waiting.

SERMON

I.

Let us open to the *Book of Is*,
which is a book of the unraveling
body, of sleepy threats from air and water
to return. It is a book of sandpaper and awe
never meant for tragically ordinary eyes.
We will read by turning
wrists: hold hands now, recall
blood's cadence in palms,
the umpteenth coming
of man as sound, as string whose timbre
makes brief, untrained eavesdroppers
of saints. In our story for today:
God spoke these words
to man—"I am changed"—man called
to God—"I cannot"—and in rage
toppled all sundials' talonous spikes,
laid each tree supine to leave no mark
of the sun or its coded passing. Man could not bear
knowing time, how long he must live under a new pain,
a pact aside from the simple first—more
than grunted lectures from gravity,
from suffocating clay to the hard
dust of his bones. By night, fixed notes
against the sky decomposed into the first few
bars of a god-silent era. What sense
man had was left in the hands—
the roughness of the word made muscle
and hide, infused in dead-
wood and stone. His task,
to begin building the book,
thinking it good. He would not finish.

It stays these forms in a posture of falling,
A pose named for a national bird
Of prey. Forms float like people
Though they are merely skins
Buoyant with lack of Is. When the water exhausts,
Those who saw no exit will be carried
Into tomorrow as trees—a second life
With the same unmistakable fate. Those
Who stayed to wade with loved ones, to end
Together, they knit a new DNA—a genetic knot
Insoluble in the blare of warnings or wind.

Those who gave speeches—the gyre
Safely north of low-relief lands—
Their sons and grandchildren will return
To carve crest into the new trees, charged,
As the powerful are, to conquer
Time. Cut letters will scar in the bark—
Thick as lips at their edges. Trees will speak
The land's old mumblings, a frequency
Beasts catch in their teeth and hairs. The people
Will not know to listen to the trees whose expression-
Less, beckoning arms take centuries to finish
An ominous wave. A godless process,
Trunks will be quartered, transmuted into homes
Thrice the size of those once owned
By the bodies who were people
But now become trees brushed onto the flat pulp
Of the *Book of Is*—a verse of one-eyed storms
That never lose a staring match with man.

(4) GROUND UP

ELEGY FOR "THE FAIR ONE"

Dear Larry,

   They've outlawed our dance—the one
we never rehearsed once but wove into
with ego's imprecision. I could have been
a better partner—me and all I learned
of brawling from my grandmother: how to
break noses, how to slip an ambush
by flooring the boy paying your fists
little attention, then letting fear
bloody the remaining mob's resolve.

   But you, I just held you like the "punk
bitch" I was. I waited
for your wildest swing—so fierce
you had no choice but to be *open*—
and I collapsed around your shoulders and neck,
your head tucked like a burden of pig hide
and air in my arm, your rage
deflating as I spun you.

"The fair one" was a slang term for a fair fight, one-on-one with no weapons.
It was often used in the phrase "Why don't y'all shoot the fair one, then?"

TOUR

The glass-bottom poem
floats on poured stone
surfaces. The windows
set in its belly
show you nothing—
no arks, ancient relics,
or species paved over. No
more reason to bury here.
People are smallest
shadows of the city. The city
realizes the city and must
forget itself to the ground
to dream its hereafter,
sparkling. SEE THE PIPES
OF YESTERDAY—that is all
the poem can offer.
If you must see ruin, glance
around, then step out quickly.
Remember, resole your feet
with the largest notes you carry
lest you disturb the city's
voracious slumber.

CALIBAN

AUGUST 21, 2004

Now two blocks from Harvard Square, I spy
my first black man since tipping a Nigerian
doorkeep for directions to Boston Common.
This shiny, beige-capped man of Windbreaker skins
debates a beggar over agency—the ability to seed
change. In the time it takes to pass them,
this show depreciates to

Just shut up	La La LA La
Fucking shut up	la la la la
Dammit shut	LA LA LA ...
the fuck	. . . .

A couple walking closer halts stride.
Master: *Performance art, maybe?*
Misses: *O, oh no! Turn around. I refuse
to be shot my last night in Cambridge.* [Insert gun
assault statistics for Harvard Square, 2004.]

This town slips me its epiphany like a secret
hand signal—the rarity of black men peculiar,
grand. Around me, brown pilgrims whisper
convenience of love "outside the race."
Whatever barbs I intend to ask them now pierce me—
the otherlust, that urge to take
towns like these in one night. I cock my mouth
to rattle back at anything. *Are you a student?*
(flattered) "No, I'm a writer." *Do you
have this sweatshirt in green?* (defensive) "I wouldn't
know. I'm a writer." *Oh, you're not a student?*
(haughty) "I'm a writer." For once

I'll wear my art, donning the exotic
trouble of black Brahmans—
find an Indian girl a shade, dare two,
lighter than me to pour myself
into seducing. Proud parents
just a few hours departed from Logan,
we could dance until only her spartan dorm room
remains open and have the kind of sex
that convinces people of love—the kind you wish
not had with those you fancy deeper.
But passing Dawes Island into Cambridge Common,
it's clear the damp grass would better suit—in the thickset
dark between foggy cones of light. There, it would be
most fitting if in the end I bid her good-bye
as silently as I say good-bye to the T.

I circle back through Harvard Yard.
A traveling man begs directions. "Wouldn't know,"
I say. "I'm just a floating head."

Back on Massachusetts, my temples pulse
a reminder—*All you have to do*
is find her. I rehearse like a door-to-door
before landing on restaurant row:
"Are you a student here?" . . . "Me? No, I'm a writer."
. . . "How long have you . . . ?" . . . "What's
your name?" . . . "Is this the usual
spot?" . . . "A place you hang out." . . . "The music,
it's alright . . . I mean, I might like it
better if you danced with me."

EYE WADING

Beneath sparse froth,
leaves of sunken shrubs flutter south
—the addling like Siren fingers—

while birds' quick, lambent browns
comb over the river, playing
Icarus-and-the-sun with its waters.

Are they scavengers like us, simply taken
with their dark reflections?
Who needs to know? I never question
why fish, like the one contorting below,
leap out from their cool medium—feeling
fortunate if it happens and I am there
to witness. These rivers, their wet
filibusters bent to marks of inquiry,

bent to cradle. This one, a contemplation
calm to the eye. Standing over its subtle churn,
the bridge reverberating under my thick soles,
I wonder how many have leapt
from here—all agrin, arms flailing—
and pierced the restless skin
in need of an answer?

LETTER HOME I

VIA LEWISBURG, PENNSYLVANIA

The town's trademarks are its streetlamps, two
Of the three orbs droop towards the earth—

Dead insects inside settle at the bottom,
Tragic pupils.

In my ambling I saw the remains
Of a barn—a gentler stop along underground rail

(So reads the sign). I always stumble
Upon these things, like the slave graves

Suffocated by dorms below Mr. Jefferson's
University. As then, I didn't know how to be present.

Of course I crossed Tubman, but kept on—
Anxious of what I'd see if I stared too long. Right now

There's rain, sky left ajar, and the wind slipping
Jabs of lightning splayed within the clouds.

I miss the lanky apartment buildings,
    the black-lunged streets,
        my sight—through which no one images me twice.

TRAIN DIALOGUE

Stranger: (*balancing his checkbook, stopping abruptly*)
Excuse me, I have to get some coffee.
Would you like a cup?

Me: (*caught off guard*)
No, no thank you.

(*stranger returns, silence
for twenty minutes*)

Me: Do you have the time?

German Stranger: It tiz eight thurty,
do you have a meeting?

Me: I have to be in Manassas by nine.

German Stranger from Charlottesville: I make zis trip a lot.
You should be zere on
time, do you have a
meeting?

Me: No, I am meeting a friend.

German Stranger from Charlottesville: Oh . . . well, you can
always get new friends.

SHADE TREE
EN ROUTE, VIRGINIA

CAPTION: *south*, the open
south where interstates have yet to graze: pity
those fields, stalks lax as though
anesthetized by their own green.
Always there is a lone player, a tree
set center—tee for a titan's game of golf.
At the longer pit stops, I chat up
7-Eleven clerks or old *Daisys*
selling flowers from plaster buckets.
I ask, an anthropologist fleeing
lands of asphalt, for the myth,
field mojo, or luck embedded in the common
landscape. The common response, *Can't say*
I've noticed. Clouds scatter birthmarks
on the earth while the trees stand frank,
proud likenesses of demigods—proud
even after thunder swallows itself
and a strike has left
the bark split and sizzling.

SIGHTSEEING I: PREFAB

MANASSAS, VIRGINIA

Side-mouthed, Jenna spells it: "None of this
.was here five years ago."
So prompted, I disassemble
the scape and sketch a before
(thatchy blots, unsolved ground).
It's all ashy brick now. Aluminum
siding, a bland meiosis: one shell
dividing until townhouses formed
a scar tissue over the deep-nicked earth.

She knows one person in each
settlement, quips names as we drive past.
They are all the same age, their parents
migrants of the same short span—
two generations feel like legacy in these
beltway-bleached satellites, suburbivores
farming bucolia only to raze it
for a same-city, gleaming with parking
lot lights and COMING SOON.

Buy-Alls, Paneras, Gelaterias to be plotted,
fastened to the dirt, to the liking.

SHEDDING A PIMP

PENN STATION, NEWARK, NEW JERSEY

(minutes ago

    she was crying
    —angry with the tears—
    while dragging bags between stone
    gauntlets, the new safety, afront the station.

        He moved, danced banishment—
        waist already turned up the street
        as his arms, serpentine, brushed her away.)

While this edge of Newark hugs the river,
watchers around me, having missed the street
exchange, see a white girl—mad
with cornrows and two bags—
and murmur among themselves.

I saw him dive into the loading zone
and push her from that bronze 'llac.

Whatever is wrong
she'll leave in this sponge of a lobby,
taking the first Greyhound in—
a thick wind in tow,
coaxing her exposed limbs.
When will it feel new—the skin,
solely hers again?

BOY DIES FALLING

ACADEMY SPIRES, NEWARK, NEW JERSEY

The truth is a line
no more follows time's ire
than a tiny child tailing a cat
echoes a sinking star.

Between our feigned light piled in the sky
and pedestrians' eyes bricked over
with the everyday, no one sees
stars or five-year-olds
piercing fifteen stories of weak atmosphere
before there is blacktop. Must we return
to the line—how form is trusted so.
The iron lines trilled across
high-rise panes should have held
his note :: his rigid curiosity
a shunt from boxed air to open (again
a line) he followed to brief flight.

Life will continue to fall from sky, even
the sun someday—a promised
dawn when no light above
will mean boys named Zahir—*shining,
radiant, blossoming*—will rebel
against gravity and plummet
upward as the beacon should.

SIGHTSEEING II

LOWER MANHATTAN, NEW YORK

Our eyes plane the boardwalk planks,
bodies leaned over upper-deck railing
of South Street's mall. I call myself
reading poetry, *The It Review*'s prizewinners.
The river before us asks that we revise—
carving out caesuras as teenagers
glide past; full pauses when the wind
sprints off the water to present itself.
I'm beginning to see most-high schematics,
how human's geometry
—arcs   angles   congruence—look
viewed from the empyreal loft.
Towards the street, a mime
tickles the ear of a stranger, and every hand
hoards another hand or waft of salty air.

Before resting, we went to the hole,
our steps slower there. Turning back to see
if we were whole, *here* really,
I found them stalled
at odd points of the viewing path,
as though I were dragging torn bags of students.

I decided to bring them to this pier,
unaware of how different
here could be four blocks away.

NOTICE
To the Addict Who Robbed Us on a Landscaping Job
UNIVERSITY HEIGHTS, NEWARK, NEW JERSEY

You could've tuned to greed, tried to pull out
a lawn mower or tuck weed whackers under each arm.
That leaf blower, a cooler porridge—
shoulder straps, detachable chute.
We didn't think twice as you zigzagged up the road,
mumbling to some muse. We turned our heads,
and you were wind, just like the machine on your back.

What black comic won't deem dope fiends too slippery,
but you trailed an aura-wake—heat streaks woven
across South Orange Avenue from University
Heights to the projects my mother rose in.

                    Know we could have pursued,
even bought back the power blower
(and saved ourselves) for a fix-worth
of bills. But, rightfully, you would've blown
if our rusty pickup came clanking your way.

We left it to the summer's judgment—fearing
our small boss and sour there was likely
a man brown as all of us selling you
something so sick you'd risk
stealing from we who carry axes,
stakes, and blades for a living.

(5) THE POST-SOUL
PAPERS

"Black will git you . . ."

"Yes, it will . . ."

"Yes, it will . . ."

"an' black won't . . ."

"Naw, it won't!"

"It do, Lawd . . ."

". . . an' it don't."

"Halleluiah . . . "

RALPH ELLISON

FOLK [AFFIRMATIVEAMBIVALENCE]

My people were known for their voices—how their harmony could nurse fields back from drought. Though my people amounted to but a few bars of the Nation's song, theirs was the bridge looped over and over, cross-faded until their bodies blurred. The Nation didn't know what to do with the bright streaks of my people. Obsessed with sound, the Nation drew blades and began to clear-cut my people's throats—heads and bodies left strewn like soft rubble. My people fled into the desert's sands, mastered the flame and art of birthing glass, built clear, tempered cities, and never returned. The Nation gradually outgrew my people. It loomed large, gazed upon them like children awed with ant farms—noses pressed against impervious, transparent panes. The Nation loved watching my people's industry but missed their sound and kept tapping the glass, begging them to sing once again. My people refused. They'd come to realize their voices were the only things able to make their houses shatter.

1980

Eighty-six degrees not counting
the ring lighting heaped
upon them. The king
leads with his mind,
bluffs with his fists. Can't fool
Cosell: "Ali's posturing
and talking, but not punching."

His head bobs like a sunflower
in a violent wind.

Let this match be punctuation,
for not going down
like Joe. Tight-lipped,
Holmes's skin says *I'm young, damn pretty,*
while Ali's jabs are wilted and easy
to spy—limp threads missing the needle
eye of his ex–sparring partner's nose.

Not the prize bouts, here
blows the leather storm that makes boxers—
the one they should run from
but stand for a heavy purse. Ali says,
"C'mon, hit me harder,"
and Holmes releases all latent
respect weighing down his wrists.

TESSERAE

JANUARY 16, 2006

Having woken with the long pool in mind, I dressed
and met January. To honor is to walk on this day—march
with no chorus of feet. Holiday gas, holiday money,
all burn in America's engine. The fire, they say,
keeps us free. Red and wet:
my nose by the time I've hoofed to Washington's
exclamation. Red, black, and green:
a *Muslim Journal* I'm tossed by the horseshoe
honoring World War II. My feet fall
between the bare trees' harmony, though,
divested, their branches all look same. I come
to reflect King, but my eyes pan for brown.
Correction: I come to be reflected—
multiplied by this prism of marble and water,
framed water mimicking sky—what is cropped
by the pool's borders might extend ad infinitum
as we. Beyond the emulsified edges of King's
image, his dream-stance on this stone,
a rich static of negroes waxing black, turning
Afro, painfully American beneath their skin.
Turn to today where we see them as one
through nostalgia's oculus. Look back,
look same. Weren't we in sync then—in step,
steeped in names of blood? There is no struggle
coded in black marrow. There is no black
marrow, simply blood and steps to spill
towards least resistance like water. History's
icy headwind fought me for this memorial
and this day's pregnant memory of merely

a blood and bone man. I win something here,
even if none like me share witness. The stone's
cold bites through my denim,
while beside me a father reads from chapped hands
the speech locked inside the stone's gray beauty
so his daughter may see herself in it—a moment
united before we all leave as strangers.

PHAT

A Metadiscourse on the Value of Canonizing the Round (Spheropygian), Broad (Platypygous), and Bulging (Pleopygian) Buttocks (with a Resistance to Such Speech)

I

Mammy is her own Madonna/whore complex, so please don't ask
if she needs help carrying *all that*. Brother Slim, you've been rapt
inside her phonetic shape for ages—save all that R&B about
wanting into them jeans, those drawers, those boots, that—

II

America's history is of not asking before helping itself to cuts of
scapedonkeyass—the strung up, disembodied curvature, a struck
sieve spilling black men who burn like phosphorous on the way
down, more flash than heat.

III

And praise be! Praise be! But what of our sister who pastor'd deem
unanointed—all there minus *that*? The one who learns to ask
God for more because the chitlin' translation states Adam named
Eve *Cola*. His descendents collect semantic royalties for life, staking
God's work is in excess which isn't excess because they see it and
it is good.

IV

The human animal will hunt what it doesn't find in mirrors, but can
convince itself of other prey when nothing near satisfies.

V

"Y'all love them Boriqua heifers 'cause they got body like black women but take your bull like white girls." So, we don't go to the parade.

VI

He wants to put his ear to her like she is all conch—mindful of the sharp tips that make her beautiful.

MCCOLLARDS

1. MISSING

See matriarchs with maroon and black caked on

like mâché. No spice racks raided,

no contents splayed about cutting boards—

the chatter that marks oven work and healing being held

low by breath nets and protocol. But before this,

the essential conflict of *fast* and *greens*. Think of the sink

plugged and burdened with a binary of emerald tops

and moss-tinted undersides, the dark, stoic water.

2. CONCEPT

The ads suggest you won't taste difference. Four for ten dollars

says your belly won't miss idioms—what aunts called

a *foot in the pot*, what you call home, served as mama's,

as seasoned to some subliminal standard. It's all synapse

and science. A green is a green is green.

Slow cooking?—we keep vats of time, tins of your mother's

silence, trucks to ship across state lines—refrigerated, quality

controlled. Prewashed, precooked crates chained up

and branded with zip codes picked fresh from the census. We aim

to give you yourself until you love it like an other.

MARTIN LUTHER KING, JR., AND HIS FAMILY: PAPER DOLLS

PLATE 1

[Martin Luther King and his wife Coretta are shown here
wearing typical underwear of the period]

Coretta doesn't know from her look—
her smile, her eye to the viewer,
the implied child. Martin
stares off at what's to come (no,
more so stares it down).

Who would see them like this?
His tee shirt, boxers, dress socks, and shoes.
Her nightgown,
heels, and pearl necklace.

Not even Hoover with his thousand
blue-maize eyes spies them
together like this.

PLATE 4

[Arrested while attempting to attend the trial of friend Ralph Abernathy,
the Kings are shown here at the police station after his arrest]

"A good break"—our fathers called it—
the pant leg buckling low
as cuff hits your shoe top.
Boys in the fifties, our fathers
grew up around men who wore suits
like the transcended wear white.

But even they could not explain
how pants break on an empty suit,
how the jacket stays taut around the shoulders,
how a hat still hovers perfectly above
lapels with no neck or head.

PLATE 7

[Coretta King's training as a vocalist was a great asset
as the wife of a minister. She wore this yellow sleeveless brocade
suit with a jeweled collar for one of her recitals]

My first love I made sure to only give
yellow roses, knowing
friendship is all that keeps.

This outfit's muffling elegance
begs Coretta tell it plain.

What form of friendship holds a song-
star in place, holds her to him through the blind
hate and crosshairs, the slapdash
traveling and the other women
standing in when she stayed to light
the way home?

She'll sing that it was something bigger.
Even love knows it's only a moon
locked in orbit by an infinitely stronger gravity.

PICCOLO BLACK ART

FOR THE ANXIOUS AMONG US

All our back-speak
tanned blue by a chiding
sun—nothing we did,
said, or asked of the day.
Within the [flesh] within those distant holds
—bodies almost living
lingua franca—all the smuggled tongue.
Within us, all the palaver stolen and run
against the grain of who we are
until sharp. Speech must prick
both ends—poison the kill
and inoculate the pred—to kill. *How*
you sound just brass and hymn?
How you sound just break
beat—no verse? Is there
one sound whole
enough to blanket-burn us
free, burn our *we* so dark
we cease to be it: no auntie,
no Rainy, no Robeson, no crunk,
no big band, no Amos, no acid,
no soul. How you sound: a moon phase
of how we sound: a permutation
of how [they] were collared
and syncopated, probed and muffled
like instruments. We play it—
Jim Crow's carcass
with holes to touch and blow,
torque the note. Must know
note whole before you can strike
and pin its wings down

in the grand book, give it name,
give it era to atrophy. How we
sound is a slow sunrise to the West.
It is not dawn yet—why worry
some shifting gleam cresting the avenue?

NOTES

OPENING
Epigraphs from "Here Is a Map of Our Country" by Adreinne Rich in *An Atlas of the Difficult World* (1991) and "Interview with Katherine Dunham" by Vèvè A. Clark in *Kaiso!: Writings by and about Katherine Dunham* (2005).

OLD SCHOOL PLAYA TO NEW SCHOOL FOOL: AN AUTHOR'S NOTE
Epigraph from "Rosa Parks" by Outkast on *Aquemini* (1998).

THE EXHIBIT: 1904 WORLD'S FAIR
Epigraph from "Changes" by N. J. Loftis in *Black Anima* (1973).

JETSAM
Epigraph from "New World Water" by Mos Def on *Black on Both Sides* (1999).

ASSEMBLY HALL
Epigraph from "It's Nation Time" by Amiri Baraka in *The LeRoi Jones / Amiri Baraka Reader* (1999).

PALINODE, ONCE REMOVED
Epigraph from *White Man, Listen!* (1956) by Richard Wright.

THE FATHER
Lines excerpted from "To Be in Love" by Gwendolyn Brooks in *Blacks* (1994).

THE POST-SOUL PAPERS
Section epigraph from *Invisible Man* (1952) by Ralph Ellison.

MARTIN LUTHER KING, JR., AND HIS FAMILY: PAPER DOLLS
Title and image captions excerpted from *Martin Luther King, Jr., and His Family: Paper Dolls* (1993) by Tom Tierney.